AI Side Hustle Millionaire Secrets

Uncover the Proven Strategies to Build a Lucrative AI Side Hustle and Retirement Passive Income

Simon E. Lee

Disclaimer

"This book is intended for informational and educational purposes only. The information presented in this book is not a substitute for professional financial or legal advice. The author and publisher make no representations or warranties of any kind, express or implied, about the completeness, accuracy, reliability, sustainability, or availability of the book or the information, products, services, or related graphics contained in the book for any purpose. You are strictly at your own risk if you place any reliance on such information."

The author may include affiliate links in this book. If you purchase a product or service through one of these links, the author may receive a commission. The presence, if any, of affiliate links does not affect the content or recommendations made in this book. The author only includes links for products or services that they believe will add value to the reader.

Dedication

To the silent multitude, the steadfast millions among

our 6.5 billion global kin, who rise with the sun to toil
and return under the cloak of night, nurturing dreams
of financial ease: this book is for you. "AI Side Hustle
Millionaire Secrets" is a tribute to your aspirations to
educate your children, to secure a life of comfort, and
to meet the myriad needs that demand your hard-
earned currency.

As the dawn of the AI Revolution breaks, it is you, the
dreamers and doers, who stand to gain from the
bounty of opportunity that this new era bestows. This
book is more than a collection of insights; it is a
beacon to guide you to shores of prosperity through
the power of AI.

May it illuminate your journey towards creating a
robust side income and a tranquil retirement. Simon

E. Lee salutes your enduring spirit and is honored to serve as your guide to harnessing the transformative potential of artificial intelligence.

This is also dedicated to my charming wife who has provided me the countless hours of latitude and space so I can finish this book.

Acknowledgments

This book stands on the shoulders of giants—the visionary tech gurus, intrepid investors, and pioneering entrepreneurs whose relentless pursuit of innovation has laid the foundation for the AI revolution. I am deeply grateful to these trailblazers who have not only envisaged a new world enhanced by artificial intelligence but have also actualized it through a plethora of AI-powered tools. They have turned science fiction into science fact, proving beyond doubt the vast potential that these technologies hold for augmenting human endeavor.

Special thanks are owed to those who, behind the scenes, developed these tools and platforms, serving as the 'proof of concept' for all to witness. Their creations are the bedrock upon which this book is built, the very instruments that will allow countless individuals to leap into the promising realm of AI side hustles.

I must also extend my heartfelt gratitude to my wife, whose unwavering support has been a beacon of inspiration. Her belief in my passion to enlighten and empower millions about the side hustle opportunities of the AI revolution has been a source of constant encouragement. Her patience and understanding have given me the space to explore and express the insights contained within these pages.

To all those mentioned and unmentioned who have played a role in this journey—I am eternally thankful. Your collective wisdom and foresight have not only shaped this work but also the future of work itself.

Preface

In an era where the whisper of Artificial Intelligence (AI) has swelled to a resounding echo across the globe, the landscape of work, income, and opportunity is being redrawn. The AI Revolution is not a distant future; it is the vivid present, an unfolding epoch that is as disruptive as it is brimming with potential. This book, "AI Side Hustle Millionaire Secrets," is a clarion call to those who have yet to awaken to the monumental shift at our doorstep.

The promise of AI is not only reserved for tech moguls or visionary entrepreneurs. It lies within reach of every individual willing to embrace the change, to learn, and to apply the secrets contained in this book. Whether you're clocking in daily to support a family, or to send your children to college, or simply working towards a more comfortable retirement, the AI Revolution brings with it a tidal wave of side hustle opportunities.

This book is a distillation of proven strategies, a guidebook to navigate the new rivers of income that AI has unleashed. It is penned with a single purpose: to equip you with the knowledge to harness AI tools and platforms, turning them into streams of additional income that could very well redefine your financial destiny.

As we stand at the cusp of transformation, the insights shared here are your map to the once-in-a-lifetime side hustle opportunities that AI offers. Let us journey through the concepts, the practical advice, and the actionable steps that can propel you from the sidelines into the heart of the AI economic revolution.

Together, let's embark on this journey to not just understand AI, but to make it work for us, ensuring that as the world changes, we are not just spectators but active participants in the wealth it can generate.

Welcome to "AI Side Hustle Millionaire Secrets." The future is not just coming; it's already here. It's time to seize it.

Simon E. Lee

Table of Contents

Introduction

"I predict that, because of artificial intelligence and its ability to automate certain tasks that in the past were impossible to automate, not only will we have a much wealthier civilization, but the quality of work will go up very significantly and a higher fraction of people will have callings and careers relative to today." ~Jeff Bezos

Artificial intelligence (AI) is one of the most transformative technologies of our time, and it is creating a once-in-a-lifetime opportunity for individuals and businesses to generate new income streams.

AI is already being used to automate a wide range of tasks, from customer service to data analysis. This is freeing up human resources to focus on more creative and strategic work.

The key to taking advantage of the unique income opportunities created by AI is to be able to identify and capitalize on emerging trends, and this book "AI Side Hustle Millionaire Secrets: Uncover the Proven Strategies to Build a Lucrative AI Side Hustle and Retirement Passive Income" will be your guide to help you do just that.

This book will provide you with the knowledge and skills you need to:

- Understand the latest AI trends and emerging applications.

- Identify AI opportunities that are relevant to your skills and interests.

- Develop a plan to launch and grow your AI side hustle.

- Monetize your AI skills and knowledge.

- Build a passive income stream from AI.

Whether you are a beginner or an experienced AI professional, this book will help you take advantage of the unique income opportunities created by AI and achieve your financial goals.

Here are some specific ways that this book can help you:

- Identify promising AI niches: This book will provide you with a comprehensive overview of the different AI niches that are ripe for disruption. You will learn about the key trends in each niche, as well as the opportunities for entrepreneurs.

- Develop a winning AI business model: This book will teach you how to develop a business model that is tailored to the unique needs of the AI market. You will learn how to identify your target market, develop a value proposition, and set pricing.

- Build a killer AI product or service: This book will provide you with the tools and resources you need to develop a high-quality AI product or service. You will learn about the different AI technologies available, as well as how to design and develop AI-powered solutions.

- Launch and market your AI business: This book will teach you how to launch and market your AI business effectively. You will learn how to build a website, create marketing materials, and generate leads.

- Monetize your AI skills and knowledge: This book will provide you with a variety of strategies for monetizing your AI skills and knowledge. You will learn how to sell your services as a freelancer, start your own AI consulting business, or build an AI-powered product or service that you can sell to others.

- Build a passive income stream from AI: This book will teach you how to build a passive income stream from AI. You will learn how to create AI-powered products and services that generate recurring revenue, such as subscription services or AI-powered software as a service (SaaS) products. This requires a deep understanding of AI technology and the industries that are being disrupted.

By following the advice in this book and taking action, you can position yourself to take advantage of the unique income opportunities created by AI and achieve your financial goals.

Why is taking consistent action as soon as possible important? The reason is consistent daily action will help keep the momentum of your side hustle building on itself until it comes to fruition!

The AI landscape is constantly changing, and the early movers have a significant advantage. By taking action now, you can position yourself to capitalize on the latest trends and developments.

Here are just a few reasons why taking action right away is important:

- The market is still small. This means there is less competition and more opportunity for early adopters.

- The technology is still evolving. This means there is a lot of room for innovation.

- The demand is growing rapidly. Businesses are increasingly looking for ways to use AI to improve their operations, products and services.

If you wait too long to take action, you may find yourself playing catch-up with the competition. Each chapter that follows will provide you with key takeaways or actionable steps to build and sustain the momentum of your profitable side hustle venture.

Chapter 1:

Understanding AI:
Beyond the Hype

"AI is the new electricity." - Andrew Ng, AI Expert

(From various interviews and talks)

Artificial Intelligence (AI) has transcended beyond

the walls of science fiction to become a dynamic and

central part of our contemporary reality. The term 'AI'

can conjure images of sentient robots or

supercomputers overthrowing humanity, but the

actuality is both more mundane and more profound.

AI is a suite of technologies, from machine learning

algorithms to natural language processing, that allows

machines to sense, comprehend, and act—and learn

autonomously. This technology is not an arcane

science but an accessible tool available to

entrepreneurs across the globe.

Understanding AI begins with demystifying its

capabilities and limitations. It's not a silver bullet; it's a

powerful lever to amplify human potential. To harness

AI, one must grasp the basics of data inputs,

algorithmic processing, and output applications.

Recognizing the distinction between Narrow AI, which

is designed to perform specific tasks, and General AI,

an intellect that rivals human cognition, is essential.

This knowledge sets the stage for exploring how AI

can be integrated into business operations to

streamline efficiency, enhance customer experiences, and open new avenues for innovation.

The AI Economy: A Landscape of Opportunity

We stand at the precipice of the AI Economy, a burgeoning ecosystem where AI is the driver of value creation and economic growth. AI's role in the economy is multifaceted—it's a product and service enhancer, a productivity booster, and a creator of new markets and job roles. As AI technology advances, it paves the way for novel business models and disrupts traditional market structures.

The AI Economy is marked by its potential for scalability and reduced marginal costs. AI systems improve with exposure to more data, enabling businesses to scale at unprecedented rates. Furthermore, the democratization of AI tools means that they are no longer the exclusive domain of tech giants; they are now accessible to small and medium-sized enterprises, leveling the playing field and offering a competitive edge.

Navigating this landscape requires understanding the sectors ripe for AI integration, such as healthcare, finance, and customer service. Entrepreneurs who can identify AI opportunities within these sectors and align them with consumer needs are positioned to capture significant value. As with any technological revolution, the AI Economy also presents challenges, including job displacement and privacy concerns, which must be navigated with foresight and ingenuity.

AI Success Stories: Lessons from Millionaires

The annals of AI are already filled with tales of success that aspiring entrepreneurs can learn from. AI millionaires are not a monolith; they are diverse individuals who have harnessed AI's power to disrupt industries, create unparalleled user experiences, and optimize operations to near perfection.

These pioneers have several traits in common. They have an unwavering belief in the transformative power of AI, a commitment to continuous learning and improvement, and the tenacity to push through failures. They understand that AI is a tool to augment human intelligence and creativity, not replace it.

Studying these success stories reveals patterns: successful AI ventures often start with addressing a clear, specific pain point. They rely on data as a critical asset and prioritize the acquisition of high-quality, structured data to train their algorithms. They also emphasize the user experience, ensuring that their AI solutions are intuitive and seamless for the end-user. Learning from these trailblazers, one can distill actionable principles for building a thriving AI-driven business.

Aligning AI with Your Financial Goals

AI can be a catalyst for achieving financial prosperity, but it requires a strategic approach to align with your financial objectives. Whether your goal is to build a steady stream of passive income, diversify your investment portfolio, or launch a scalable startup, AI can provide the leverage needed to accelerate your journey.

The first step is to define clear financial targets and assess how AI can contribute to these goals. This might involve automating tasks to save time and costs, utilizing AI-driven analytics for smarter decision-making, or creating AI-powered products that address market gaps.

Financial goals also dictate the scale and scope of AI implementation. Bootstrapped projects might start with simple automation tools, while more ambitious ventures may require significant investment in custom AI solutions. Regardless of the scale, the key is to start small, measure the impact, and iteratively refine the approach.

An important aspect is to ensure that the ROI of AI integration is measured against defined financial goals. This not only includes direct revenue increases but also cost savings, customer lifetime value enhancements, and improved competitive positioning. By maintaining a laser focus on financial outcomes, entrepreneurs can make informed decisions about where and how to invest in AI.

Ethics and AI: Building a Responsible Side Hustle

In an era where AI is becoming a cornerstone of business strategy, ethical considerations must be at the forefront. Building a responsible AI side hustle is not just about compliance with laws and regulations; it's about fostering trust and ensuring fairness, transparency, and accountability in AI systems.

Ethical AI involves the deliberate design of algorithms that avoid biases, respect privacy, and promote inclusivity. It means being transparent about how AI systems make decisions and how data is used. Entrepreneurs must take a proactive stance on ethical issues, anticipating potential moral dilemmas and societal impacts before they arise.

Incorporating ethics into your AI business model is also smart economics. Consumers are increasingly aware of and concerned about AI ethics. They are more likely to engage with companies that demonstrate a commitment to responsible AI practices. Moreover, ethical lapses can lead to public relations disasters and legal challenges that could threaten the very survival of a business.

Building a responsible AI side hustle, then, is about embedding ethical principles into the fabric of your business strategy. It requires ongoing vigilance and a commitment to doing right by all stakeholders involved—customers, employees, and the broader society.

Remember the Key Takeaways from This Chapter

If you've journeyed with us through this chapter, you've already taken your first bold steps into the vibrant world of AI and the boundless opportunities it brings. Let's lock in the key takeaways from our adventure together and keep the momentum going!

First off, we've seen that AI isn't just for tech whizzes or sci-fi fans—it's a real and present tool that's reshaping our world. We're not talking about robots taking over; we're talking about smart, practical technologies that amplify your capabilities, make you more efficient, and can even make you look like a genius to your customers.

Remember, the AI Economy is not a far-off concept; it's here, and it's packed with opportunities that are ripe for the picking. It's like a playground for entrepreneurs where the swings and slides are made of data, algorithms, and automation tools. Jump on and enjoy the ride, but don't forget to play nice with regulations and stay ahead of the curve.

We also dove into some incredible success stories, didn't we? These are the people who've ridden the AI wave to the shores of Millionaire Island. They aren't superheroes—they're folks like you and me who saw the power of AI and grabbed it with both hands.

They've shown us that with the right mindset and a dash of daring, the AI tide can lift all boats.

Now, aligning AI with your financial goals is like tuning a guitar. Get it right, and you'll make beautiful music—make wealth, in our case. So set those goals, find your AI tune, and start strumming. Small steps lead to big leaps in the financial concerto of life.

And ethics—oh, that's the heart of the matter. Building an AI side hustle without ethics is like baking a cake without sugar—sure, it's a cake, but who wants it? Be the baker who uses the best ingredients, bakes with care, and serves up a slice of trust with every piece. That's how you win hearts and wallets.

As we close this chapter, hold onto these nuggets of wisdom. They're your passport to the AI realm, your map to treasures untold. So take a deep breath, gear up with these insights, and let's set sail to the next chapter. The winds of AI are in our sails, my friend, and they're blowing us straight to success!

Your Call to Action

Now that you've learned about the key takeaways of this chapter, it's time to take action. Here are some ideas to get you started:

- Identify your AI niche. What are your skills and interests? What problems can AI help you solve? Once you know your niche, you can start to develop a business plan.

- Set your financial goals. How much money do you want to make with your AI side hustle? Once you know your goals, you can start to develop a strategy for achieving them.

- Be ethical. Use AI in a way that benefits society and doesn't harm others. This will help you build trust with your customers and make your business more successful.

Here are some specific steps you can take today:

- List your skills and interests.

- Brainstorm AI-powered products or services that you could create.

- Research your target market and identify their needs.

- Develop a business plan.

- Start building your AI product or service.

- Market and launch your AI product or service.

Remember, the AI Economy is full of opportunities. With the right mindset and a dash of daring, you can achieve your financial goals and make a positive impact on the world.

Let's set sail for success!

Chapter 2:

Laying the Foundation for Your AI Side Hustle

"Artificial intelligence will reach human levels by around 2029. Follow that out further to, say, 2045, we will have multiplied the intelligence, the human biological machine intelligence of our civilization a billion-fold." - Ray Kurzweil, Author and Futurist (Interview with PBS, Feb. 3, 2011)

We're about to lay down some serious groundwork for your AI side hustle. Imagine you're an architect sketching out a blueprint. This chapter is just that—

the blueprint of your future success. So sharpen your pencils, or rather, get your fingers ready to tap

awa y on your keyb oard

, beca use we'r e

starting with the nuts and bolts that will hold up your AI empire!

Essential AI Terminology and Concepts

Dive into the language of AI, and you'll find it's not just jargon; it's the alphabet of tomorrow. Understand what AI, machine learning, deep learning, and neural networks mean, and you'll start seeing the matrix of possibilities. Think of it like learning the language before visiting a new country – it can transform your experience entirely!

It's not about mastering complex equations or coding overnight. Get the gist of terms like 'algorithmic bias,' 'data mining,' and 'natural language processing.' These aren't just fancy words; they're the keys to unlock the secrets of AI. By familiarizing yourself with these concepts, you're putting on your gear before diving into the ocean of AI opportunities. Ready to get fluent in AI?

Identifying Your Niche in the AI Market

The AI market is a grand buffet with endless options, but success comes when you fill your plate with what suits your taste—and expertise. Identifying your niche is like picking your favorite dessert; it should excite you and suit your unique flavor.

To find your niche, look at where your passions intersect with market needs. Are you fascinated by AI in healthcare, or does the thought of AI-powered finance solutions make your heart race? Research, observe, and listen to what the market whispers (or sometimes shouts). That's where you'll find your sweet spot.

Remember, a niche is not a life sentence; it's the starting block of your AI marathon. Choose wisely, but don't be afraid to pivot as you learn and grow. Your niche is your beacon; let it guide you through the vast AI seas.

Building a Knowledge Base: Resources and Learning

Building your AI knowledge base is like assembling your very own Iron Man suit. You need the best pieces—not all the pieces—to make something powerful. There are oceans of resources out there, from online courses, webinars, e-books to AI boot camps. Find the ones that fit your learning style and schedule.

You don't need a PhD to get started; you just need a curious mind and the commitment to learn. Every article read, every tutorial watched, and every experiment conducted adds a piece to your armor. Focus on practical skills that will serve your niche and aim to understand the theory that will empower your decisions.

Build a learning routine and stick to it. Even 15 minutes a day adds up to over 90 hours a year of learning! Think of it as daily compound interest on your knowledge investment. Before you know it, you'll be the Tony Stark of your AI niche!

Legal Considerations: Compliance and Protections

Venturing into AI without considering the legal landscape is like building a castle on quicksand—it won't stand for long. Compliance is your fortress. Understand data protection laws, intellectual property rights, and contractual obligations.

Your AI tool could be the next big thing, but if it's not legally sound, it might never see the light of day. Get cozy with terms like GDPR, CCPA, or copyright law. They may seem like hurdles, but they're actually the guardrails that keep your venture on the road to longevity and trust.

Consider consulting a legal eagle who specializes in tech startups. Yes, it's an investment, but think of it as the armor plating on your Iron Man suit. It's not just about protecting your own creation; it's about respecting the digital landscape and the users who inhabit it.

Crafting a Business Plan for Your AI Venture

No treasure map leads to success without X marking the spot. Your business plan is that map, and X marks your goals. Crafting a business plan is like drawing the treasure map for your AI side hustle—both an exciting and critical process.

Detail your vision, market research, and monetization strategy. Who are your customers? How will you reach them? What's your revenue model? These aren't just sections of a document; they're chapters of your upcoming success story.

Think of your business plan as a living document. It will grow and evolve as your understanding of the AI market deepens. When it's time to seek investment, your business plan will speak for you, telling the compelling tale of your upcoming venture.

Make Your Key Takeaways Your Mantra

As we wrap up this chapter, let's tuck these key points into our toolbelt:

Mastering AI terminology is your first step to thinking like an AI entrepreneur.
Your niche is your north star—find it, follow it, and if necessary, recalibrate.
Building a knowledge base is non-negotiable. Invest time in learning to yield returns in earnings.

Don't sidestep legalities. They're the backbone of your business's credibility.

A dynamic business plan is your roadmap. Draft it, refine it, and let it guide you.

Take a moment to celebrate; you've just fortified the foundation of your AI side hustle. With this robust base, you're poised to build something incredible. Ready to turn the page? Let's keep the momentum going and dive into the next chapter—your future self will thank you!

Your Call to Action

Now that you have the foundation of AI entrepreneurship under your belt, it's time to start building your AI side hustle.

Here are some actionable steps to get you started:

- Master AI terminology. This will help you communicate effectively with other AI professionals and understand the latest trends and developments in the field.

- Identify your niche. What problems can AI help you solve? Who is your target market? Once you know your niche, you can start to develop specific products or services.

- Build a knowledge base. Learn as much as you can about AI technology and the specific AI applications that are relevant to your niche. This will help you make informed decisions and develop high-quality products and services.

- Stay up-to-date on legalities. Make sure you comply with all applicable laws and regulations. This includes things like data privacy and intellectual property rights.

- Create a dynamic business plan. This will help you stay focused and on track as you build your AI side hustle. Be sure to update your business plan regularly as your business grows and evolves.

Taking these steps will help you build a successful AI side hustle that achieves your financial goals and makes a positive impact on the world.

Now, turn the page and start your journey to becoming an AI entrepreneur!

Chapter 3:

Understanding AI Tools and Technologies

"Artificial Intelligence is the tool of the technological mind." - Ginni Rometty, Former CEO of IBM (Interview with CNBC, 2018)

Embarking on a journey into the AI landscape
without understanding the tools and technologies at
your disposal would be like trying to paint a
masterpiece without knowing your brushes and
colors. This chapter is the studio where you'll become
acquainted with the essentials that will allow you to
paint your entrepreneurial picture with broad,
confident strokes. With the right tools, technologies,
and a bit of creativity, you're not just ready to join the
AI revolution—you're ready to lead it.

Whether you're a seasoned techie or someone who
just recently figured out how to set up an email

signature, this chapter is for you. You'll learn how to select the best AI platforms, understand the magic behind machine learning algorithms, and become a maestro of data. We'll also share some neat automation tools to make your side hustle run smoother than a jazz ensemble. And because AI doesn't stand still, we'll teach you how to keep up with the trends. Buckle up; it's going to be an enlightening ride!

AI Platforms: Choosing the Right One for You

AI platforms are like cars: you need to find one that suits your style, needs, and budget. There's a myriad to choose from—some are the flashy sports cars that promise speed and performance, while others are reliable SUVs designed for a variety of tasks. Deciding on the right platform is pivotal in how you will navigate the AI terrain.

Do you need something user-friendly like Google's AI Platform, or are you looking for the robustness of IBM

Watson? Perhaps the flexibility of Microsoft Azure appeals to your entrepreneurial spirit. Explore your options, take them for a test drive, and don't be shy to ask around. Your choice of platform will either be the launchpad for your success or a lesson in what not to choose next time.

Demystifying Machine Learning Algorithms

Machine learning algorithms are the secret sauce to AI's success, but they're not as enigmatic as they seem. Think of them as recipes that, when followed, create delightful dishes out of your data. Some recipes are simple—perfect for beginners—while others are more complex, designed for the gourmet data chefs.

Understanding the basics, like regression analysis for predictions or clustering for finding patterns, can go a long way. It's not necessary to memorize them all; just recognize them on the menu and know which dish to serve for what occasion. It's this understanding that will elevate your AI dishes from mere fast food to gourmet feasts.

Leveraging Data: Collection and Analysis

Data is the currency in the AI market, and how you collect and analyze it can make or break your venture. Learning to leverage data is like learning to find and pan for gold. You'll discover there's often more than glitters on the surface, and the real value comes from knowing what to look for and how to polish it.

Get to grips with the tools for data collection, from online surveys to web scraping, and understand the analytics that will help you transform raw data into insights. Your ability to collect and analyze data is what will set your AI side hustle apart from the hobbyists.

Automation Tools to Streamline Your Hustle

The right automation tools can make your AI side hustle as slick as a Vegas card dealer. They're the little helpers that work behind the scenes, making sure your business runs like clockwork. From scheduling social media posts to automating customer service with chatbots, these tools are the trusty sidekicks to your superhero venture.

Explore different automation tools and consider which mundane tasks they can take off your hands. The goal is to work smarter, not harder. With more time to focus on strategy and growth, your side hustle will soon be playing in the big leagues.

Staying Ahead: Tracking AI Trends

In the fast-paced world of AI, trends can be as fleeting as fashion—what's in today might be out tomorrow. Staying ahead of the game is about keeping your finger on the pulse of innovation. Subscribe to AI newsletters, follow thought leaders on social media, and join online forums where the latest trends are as hotly debated as the latest episode of a hit series.

Being trend-savvy will help you anticipate changes, adapt your strategies, and innovate ahead of your competition. Think of it as having a crystal ball that gives you a sneak peek into the future of AI.

Weave Your Key Takeaways Into Your AI Side Hustle Fabric.

Here's the cheat sheet to what we've covered:

Choosing the right AI platform is a foundational decision—weigh your options carefully.
Machine learning algorithms are less mystique, and more method—learn the methods.
Data collection and analysis are your treasure maps—learn to read them well.
Automation tools are your silent partners—embrace them to boost productivity.
Trend tracking keeps you at the forefront—stay informed to stay ahead.

By now, you should feel more familiar with the tools and technologies that will serve as the building blocks for your AI side hustle. With the right tools in your belt, you're ready to construct a future that not only meets your financial goals but exceeds them.

Your Actionable Step to Keep the Momentum

Now that you have a better understanding of the tools and technologies involved in AI side hustles, it's time to put your knowledge into action. Here are some specific steps you can take:

- Choose an AI platform. There are many different AI platforms available, each with its own strengths and weaknesses. Do some research to find a platform that is right for your needs and budget.

- Learn about machine learning algorithms. Machine learning algorithms are the foundation of AI. Learn about different types of algorithms and how they are used to solve different problems.

- Collect and analyze data. Data is the fuel that powers AI. Start collecting data that is relevant to your AI side hustle. You can use this data to train your machine-learning algorithms and develop insights.

- Automate tasks. Automation tools can help you save time and boost productivity. Identify tasks in your AI side hustle that can be automated, and find tools that can help you automate them.

- Track trends. AI is a rapidly evolving field. It's important to stay up-to-date on the latest trends and developments. This will help you make informed decisions and keep your AI side hustle competitive.

By following these steps, you can build a successful AI side hustle that achieves your financial goals and makes a positive impact on the world.

So what are you waiting for? Start building your AI future today!

Take action now to help ensure your AI side hustle success!

Chapter 4:

Developing Your AI Product or Service

"The automation of factories has already decimated jobs in traditional manufacturing, and the rise of artificial intelligence is likely to extend this job destruction deep into the middle classes, with only the most caring, creative, or supervisory roles remaining."
- Stephen Hawking, Theoretical Physicist (Reddit AMA, July 27, 2015)

The thrilling journey of creating an AI product or

service is akin to sculpting a masterpiece from a block of marble. With the right vision and tools, what starts as a rough idea can  transform into something of great value and beauty. This chapter is about chipping away at the superfluous, honing in on the essentials, and revealing the innovation within. As we explore the stages of product development, from the seed of an idea to a fully-fledged market offering, remember that every successful entrepreneur once stood exactly where you stand now: at the precipice of creation, ready to take the plunge.

It's time to roll up your sleeves and get your hands dirty in the creative process. By the end of this chapter, you'll have a blueprint for developing an AI product or service that not only meets a market need but does so with panache. Let's turn that spark of an idea into a roaring fire of innovation.

Ideation: Brainstorming AI Solutions

Ideation is the creative process of generating, developing, and communicating new ideas. It's where all great AI products or services begin their journey. Whether it's a spark that comes to you in the shower or a concept that's been brewing in the back of your mind for years, this is where that germ of an idea starts to take shape.

Dive into brainstorming sessions without inhibitions. Use techniques like mind mapping or SWOT analysis to flesh out your thoughts. Consider what problems you want to solve and how AI can be harnessed to address them. Think about what makes your idea unique and how it will stand out in the crowded marketplace. The key is to think big, start small, and begin now.

Designing Your MVP (Minimum Viable Product)

The MVP is your hypothesis in physical (or digital) form. It's the bare-bones version of your product, built to test the most basic assumptions about your market. Designing an MVP requires you to distill your vision down to its essence. What is the core functionality that solves the problem? Resist the urge to add bells and whistles—focus on the necessity, not the nicety.

In this lean form, your MVP will be the test pilot for your idea, soaring into the hands of early users and collecting invaluable data. Keep it simple, make it functional, and let it loose swiftly. The MVP is not the end game; it's the starting block.

User Experience (UX) Principles for AI

User Experience in AI isn't just about how your product looks; it's about how it feels and operates. Good UX is like a good conversation—it flows naturally, it's engaging, and it meets expectations. It's about creating a product that users can interact with intuitively, without a second thought.

Apply UX principles to ensure that your AI product is accessible, usable, and delightful to interact with. Remember, AI should enhance the experience, not complicate it. Conduct user research, build personas, and craft user journeys that will inform the design decisions you make. An AI product with stellar UX is more than smart; it's wise.

Prototyping and Testing Your AI Model

Prototyping is where your idea starts to look and feel like a real product. It's an exploratory phase, allowing you to understand the intricacies of your AI model and interface. Testing, on the other hand, is the rigorous process of poking and prodding your prototype to expose its weaknesses and strengths.

In this stage, be prepared to fail fast and learn faster. Use the feedback to refine your AI model and user interface. Iterative prototyping and testing are the pulses that keep your product's development alive and kicking. They transform good ideas into great products through relentless refinement.

Iterating to Success: Feedback and Improvements

Iteration is the heartbeat of innovation. It's about using feedback to evolve your product continuously. Embrace user feedback, whether it's praise that boosts your confidence or criticism that cuts to the core. Both are invaluable.

Treat each piece of feedback as a stepping stone towards success. Iterate your product by enhancing what works and revamping what doesn't. It's a cycle of never-ending improvement that propels your product from being merely functional to truly phenomenal.

Cheer Yourself on with these Key Takeaways

As we wrap up this chapter, let's reflect on the essential steps of AI product development:

Ideation is where everything begins; never underestimate the power of a well-nurtured idea.

The MVP is your reality check—build it to test and validate your market fit.
UX in AI is your silent ambassador—invest in it.

Prototyping and testing are where theoretical meets practical—get tangible, get data, get better.

Iteration is where good becomes great—listen, learn, and evolve.

Embed these key takeaways into your entrepreneurial mindset, and let them guide you as you develop your AI product or service. Remember, in the world of AI, the only constant is change. Be flexible, be receptive, and let the journey shape both you and your product for the better.

Your Actionable Steps

Now that you have a good understanding of the essential steps of AI product development, it's time to start taking action. Here are five specific steps you can take:

- Ideate: Brainstorm AI product ideas and evaluate them based on their potential impact, feasibility, and market fit.

- Build an MVP: Develop a minimum viable product (MVP) to test your idea and validate your market fit.

- Invest in UX: Design a user experience that is intuitive, engaging, and accessible to your target audience.

- Prototype and test: Create a prototype of your AI product and test it with users to get feedback and iterate on your design.

- Iterate and improve: Continue to iterate on your AI product based on user feedback and market data.

By following these steps, you can develop an AI product that is successful, user-friendly, and meets the needs of your target market.

Remember, the AI landscape is constantly changing, so it's important to be flexible and adaptable. By following these tips, you can position yourself for success in the world.

Chapter 5:

Monetizing Your AI Side Hustle

"Artificial intelligence will revolutionize every aspect of our lives and create more wealth than anything that's come before." - Mark Cuban, Investor and Entrepreneur (Interview with Bloomberg, March 24, 2018)

Congratulations! You've conceptualized, developed,

and polished your AI product or service. Now, we approach the pivotal phase where your creation starts yielding financial fruits. Monetizing a side hustle isn't just about making money—it's about crafting a value proposition so compelling that your customers will be happy to pay for it.

This chapter will navigate through the art and science of turning your AI side hustle into a profitable venture.

Whether you're aiming for a steady stream of supplemental income or dreaming big to hit that millionaire mark, the monetization strategies we discuss here will be your guide.

In this journey from concept to cash, we'll look at how to price your AI solutions, market them effectively, optimize for conversions, and build a loyal customer base. We'll also explore how to scale your hustle without losing the personal touch that makes small ventures special. With each step, your confidence as a tech-savvy entrepreneur will solidify, as will your bank balance.

Pricing Strategies for AI Offerings

Pricing is not just a number—it's a communicator of value. For AI offerings, pricing strategies must reflect the innovation, efficiency, and cutting-edge tech that your product or service embodies. It's a delicate balance between perceived value and market demand.

Consider various models, from one-time purchases and subscription-based models to freemium approaches with premium features. Evaluate your costs, understand your customer's willingness to pay, and scrutinize your competitors' pricing. The right strategy will not only cover your costs and generate profit but also anchor your product's position in the market. Remember, the goal is profitability with sustainability.

Marketing Your AI Product or Service

Marketing is storytelling where your AI product is the protagonist. How will you narrate its tale? Begin with understanding your audience—know their needs, desires, and pain points. Craft your messaging to resonate with them, showcasing how your AI solution makes their life easier or business more profitable.

Use targeted marketing strategies that leverage SEO, content marketing, and social media campaigns. In the digital age, an effective online presence is invaluable. Be clear, be honest, and be exciting. After all, you're not just selling a product; you're offering a doorway to the future.

Sales Funnels and Conversion Optimization

A sales funnel is the journey you design for potential customers, guiding them from first contact to final purchase. Every step in this funnel should be optimized for conversions. Create awareness with valuable content, capture interest with lead magnets, nurture desire with benefits-focused copy, and compel action with irresistible offers.

Analyze data to understand where prospects drop off and test different approaches to improve conversion rates. The more seamless and persuasive your funnel, the better your chances of turning prospects into loyal customers.

Building a Customer Base with Social Proof

Social proof is the currency of trust in the digital marketplace. Testimonials, reviews, case studies— these are powerful tools to build credibility. Showcase the success stories of those who've benefited from your AI solution. Let their words be the wind beneath your product's wings.

Engage with customers on social platforms, collect feedback, and show potential customers that you're not just selling a product—you're creating a community of innovation and satisfaction.

Scalability: Growing Your Side Hustle

Your side hustle is a living entity; it needs room to grow. Scalability means planning for success. As demand increases, you must be able to expand without compromising on quality or customer experience.

Automation, delegation, and smart resource management are key. Keep an eye on market trends and adapt accordingly. Growth is not just about bigger profits—it's also about broader impact.

Let Your Key Takeaways Inspire You to Be the Best AI Side Hustler You Can Be

This chapter has journeyed through the monetization maze, illuminating paths to profit.

Here are your compass points:

- Price with precision to reflect value and viability.

- Market with a narrative that captivates and convinces.

- Optimize each step of the sales funnel to ensure no lead is left behind.

- Build trust through social proof, turning customers into advocates.

- Plan for scalability so that growth is a smooth transition, not a stumbling block.

Keep these takeaways close as they're the signposts to monetization success.

Chapter 6:

Branding and Positioning Your AI Business

"Machine intelligence is the last invention that humanity will ever need to make." - Nick Bostrom, Philosopher (TED Talk, 2015)

In the sea

of burgeoning technology enterprises, your AI

side hustle needs more than just a good product—it needs a personality. Branding is about imbuing your business with character and voice, making it relatable and memorable. Positioning, on the other hand, is about carving out a unique space in the market landscape where your business can not only survive but thrive. This chapter is dedicated to creating a brand that stands out and a position that delivers a competitive edge.

A strong brand evokes emotion, builds loyalty, and becomes synonymous with quality. Positioning, when done right, makes your business the go-to solution for a specific problem or need in the AI space. Let's embark on the transformative journey of branding and positioning your AI side hustle.

The Essence of Branding in AI

Your brand is your promise to your customer. It tells them what they can expect from your products and services, and it differentiates you from your competitors. With AI being a complex field, your branding should simplify the message and convey the benefits clearly and concisely. It's about connecting with your audience on an emotional level and providing them with a story they can be part of.

Crafting a Unique Value Proposition

The Unique Value Proposition (UVP) is the cornerstone of your business's identity. It's a clear statement that describes the benefit of your offer, how you solve your customer's needs, and what distinguishes you from the competition. In AI, your UVP must not only communicate the function and advantage of your technology but also its applicability and relevance to the customer.

The Power of Visual Identity in AI

In a field as intangible as AI, your visual identity gives substance to your brand. It's the colors, the logo, and the design language that become instantly recognizable to your customers. Your visual branding should reflect the innovative nature of your AI business and be versatile enough to remain relevant as the industry evolves.

Building a Narrative Around Your AI Brand

Stories are how humans connect and make sense of the world. Your AI brand's narrative should tell the story of your journey, the challenges you solve, and the future you envision. Through this narrative, you can engage your audience, instill your brand's values, and create emotional anchors that foster loyalty.

Strategic Positioning in the AI Marketplace

Positioning is about finding the right angle in the market where your brand can shine. It's a strategic effort to influence consumer perception of your brand or products in relation to competitors. In the AI market, where competition is fierce, a well-thought-out positioning strategy is crucial for capturing attention and interest.

Leveraging Content Marketing for AI

Content marketing is a strategic marketing approach focused on creating and distributing valuable, relevant, and consistent content to attract and retain a clearly defined audience. For AI businesses, content marketing is not just about promotion; it's about educating your market, providing insights, and establishing thought leadership.

Make These Key Takeaways Part of Your AI Side Hustle DNA

Brand and position your AI side hustle not just as a business but as a beacon of innovation and trust. Remember:

- Your brand is the emotional and psychological relationship you have with your customers.

- A compelling UVP is your battle cry in the crowded AI market.

- Visual identity is your flag; wave it high and proud.

- Narratives are your connective tissue with the audience; weave them with care.

- Positioning is your chess move; play it with foresight.

- Content marketing is your ongoing dialogue with the world; make it count.

With these takeaways in mind, your brand and positioning will not just define your business but also the impact it has on the AI industry.

Chapter 7:

Strategies for
Sustained Growth
and Passive Income

"The AI revolution is not coming; it's already upon us, and it's accelerating." - Kevin Kelly, Founding Executive Editor of Wired magazine (Wired, Dec. 14, 2014)

In the sea of burgeoning technology enterprises, your AI side hustle

needs more than just a good product—it needs a personality. Branding is about imbuing your business with character and voice, making it relatable and memorable.

Positioning, on the other hand, is about carving out a unique space in the market landscape where your business can not only survive but thrive. This chapter is dedicated to creating a brand that stands out and a position that delivers a competitive edge. A strong brand evokes emotion, builds loyalty, and becomes synonymous with quality. Positioning, when done right, makes your business the go-to solution for a specific problem or need in the AI space. Let's embark on the transformative journey of branding and positioning your AI side hustle.

The Essence of Branding in AI

Your brand is your promise to your customer. It tells them what they can expect from your products and services, and it differentiates you from your competitors. With AI being a complex field, your branding should simplify the message and convey the benefits clearly and concisely. It's about connecting with your audience on an emotional level and providing them with a story they can be part of.

Crafting a Unique Value Proposition

The Unique Value Proposition (UVP) is the cornerstone of your business's identity. It's a clear statement that describes the benefit of your offer, how you solve your customer's needs, and what distinguishes you from the competition. In AI, your UVP must not only communicate the function and advantage of your technology but also its applicability and relevance to the customer.

The Power of Visual Identity in AI

In a field as intangible as AI, your visual identity gives substance to your brand. It's the colors, the logo, and the design language that become instantly recognizable to your customers. Your visual branding should reflect the innovative nature of your AI business and be versatile enough to remain relevant as the industry evolves.

Building a Narrative Around Your AI Brand

Stories are how humans connect and make sense of the world. Your AI brand's narrative should tell the story of your journey, the challenges you solve, and the future you envision. Through this narrative, you can engage your audience, instill your brand's values, and create emotional anchors that foster loyalty.

Strategic Positioning in the AI Marketplace

Positioning is about finding the right angle in the market where your brand can shine. It's a strategic effort to influence consumer perception of your brand or products in relation to competitors. In the AI market, where competition is fierce, a well-thought-out positioning strategy is crucial for capturing attention and interest.

Leveraging Content Marketing for AI

Content marketing is a strategic marketing approach focused on creating and distributing valuable, relevant, and consistent content to attract and retain a clearly defined audience. For AI businesses, content marketing is not just about promotion; it's about educating your market, providing insights, and establishing thought leadership.

Let these key takeaways guide you forward!

Brand and position your AI side hustle not just as a business but as a beacon of innovation and trust.

Remember:

- Your brand is the emotional and psychological relationship you have with your customers.

- A compelling UVP is your battle cry in the crowded AI market.

- Visual identity is your flag; wave it high and proud.

- Narratives are your connective tissue with the audience; weave them with care.

- Positioning is your chess move; play it with foresight.

- Content marketing is your ongoing dialogue with the world; make it count.

With these takeaways in mind, your brand and positioning will not just define your business but also the impact it has on the AI industry.

Chapter 8:

The Future of AI and Long-Term Wealth Building

"AI is probably the most important thing humanity has ever worked on. I think of it as something more profound than electricity or fire." - Sundar Pichai, CEO of Alphabet Inc. (Interview at MSNBC, Jan. 26, 2018)

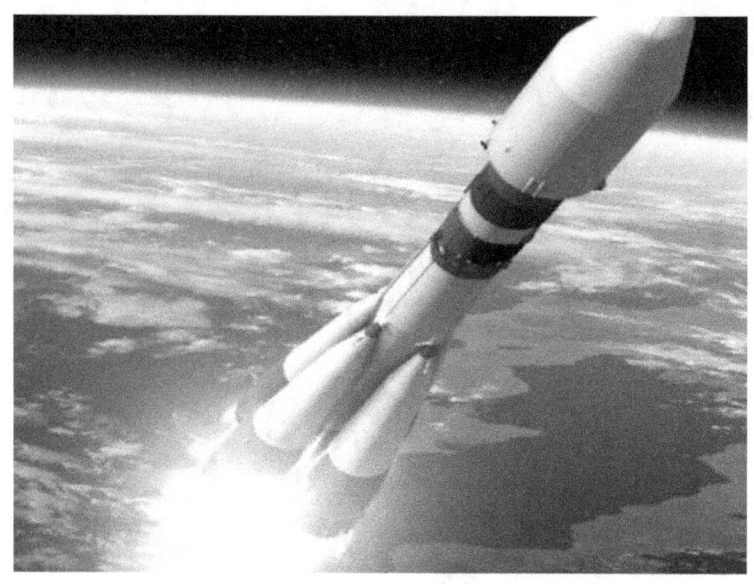

Envisioning the future of AI is not just about

predicting technological advancements; it's about
understanding the potential for these developments to
create long-term wealth. AI is a transformative force,
reshaping industries, spawning new markets, and
creating unprecedented investment opportunities.

This chapter is designed to equip you with the
foresight to capitalize on these shifts, ensuring that
your AI side hustle is not just a fleeting venture but a
cornerstone in a larger wealth-building strategy. As

we look beyond the horizon, it's about positioning yourself where the trajectory of AI aligns with sound financial planning and ethical considerations, paving the way to legacy building and financial freedom. Let's venture into the future and map out the steps to make AI a vital part of your enduring wealth.

Predicting Market Trends in AI

Understanding and predicting AI market trends is akin to having a crystal ball. Grasping where AI is headed can position you to make strategic decisions that align with future demands. It's not about chasing every trend but identifying the shifts that have staying power and align with your values and goals.

Investment Opportunities in AI and Tech Startups

The dynamic world of AI is ripe with investment opportunities. From angel investing in promising startups to crowdfunding platforms, putting your capital into innovative AI ventures can yield substantial returns. It's about recognizing potential and being part of the next big breakthrough.

Ethical Investing and Social Impact

Investing in AI is not just about financial returns; it's about contributing to a future that is ethical and beneficial for society. Ethical investing focuses on companies that prioritize social impact, ensuring that your wealth grows through means that align with your principles.

Diversification: Beyond Your AI Hustle

While your AI hustle may be at the center of your wealth-building efforts, diversification remains a cornerstone of financial stability. Explore how investing in non-AI sectors can safeguard against volatility and create a balanced investment portfolio.

Legacy Building and Financial Freedom

Your AI side hustle can be the start of a legacy that extends beyond your lifetime. It's about building assets that provide financial freedom not just for you but for future generations. This involves strategic planning, smart estate management, and a vision that transcends the immediate.

Let Your Key Takeaways Be Your North Star.

Let's distill the key insights from this chapter:

- Market trend analysis is crucial for future-proofing your AI investments.

- Tech startups present lucrative, albeit high-risk, investment frontiers.

- Ethical investing ensures your wealth contributes to positive societal change.

- Diversification is your hedge against uncertainty and market fluctuations.

- Legacy building is the ultimate manifestation of long-term wealth.

Embrace these principles as you navigate the future of AI and wealth creation.

Action Items to Nurture an "AI is My Lucrative Side-Hustle Vehicle Mindset"

As we wrap up this chapter, your action plan should center on long-term vision and continuous adaptation. Make it a habit to stay informed on AI market trends and emerging investment opportunities. Allocate time to evaluate the social impact of your investments and diversify your portfolio to protect and grow your wealth. Finally, keep the future in mind: every decision you make should be a stepping stone toward financial freedom and a lasting legacy. Let these action items be the building blocks of a mindset.

Chapter 9:

AI-Powered Tools and Software

"As more and more artificial intelligence is entering into the world, more and more emotional intelligence must enter into leadership." - Amit Ray, Pioneer of Compassionate AI Movement (Book: Compassionate Artificial Intelligence, 2018)

In the digital age, AI-powered tools and software are not just conveniences; they are essential instruments that can give your side hustle an edge in a competitive marketplace. This chapter provides a curated list of the top AI tools and software recommendations designed to enhance productivity, streamline operations, and bolster the overall efficiency of your business.

From time-saving automation to sophisticated data analysis, the right tools can transform your side hustle into a well-oiled machine capable of generating passive income with minimal intervention. Whether you are just starting out or looking to upgrade your digital toolkit, this chapter is your guide to the software that will empower you to work smarter, not harder, as you build and grow your AI-driven venture.

Overview of Essential AI Tools for Entrepreneurs

Navigating the vast landscape of AI tools can be daunting. This overview introduces you to the essential tools every AI entrepreneur should have in their arsenal, from development platforms to deployment environments. Understanding these tools will equip you with the capabilities to bring your AI concepts to fruition.

Productivity Boosters: AI for Time and Project Management

Maximize your productivity with AI tools that streamline time and project management. Explore software options that automate scheduling, task allocation, and progress tracking, freeing up your time to focus on strategic business activities.

AI-Driven Analytics and Data Visualization Tools

In a data-driven world, AI analytics and visualization tools are invaluable. They convert raw data into actionable insights, providing a clear visual representation of complex information to guide your business decisions.

Customer Relationship Management with AI

Discover how AI can revolutionize customer relationship management (CRM). From personalized communication to predictive sales data, AI-driven CRM tools help you understand and cater to your customers more effectively.

AI for Content Creation and Curation

Content is king, and AI tools can help you reign supreme. Learn about AI solutions that assist with generating, curating, and optimizing content, ensuring your message resonates with your target audience.

Financial Management and Investment Tools

Financial oversight is critical in any business. Delve into the world of AI-powered financial management and investment tools that offer real-time insights, risk assessment, and automated trading strategies.

Security and Privacy: Protecting Your Digital Assets

With great power comes great responsibility. In this subchapter, you'll learn about the importance of AI tools in safeguarding your digital assets, and ensuring the security and privacy of your business's and customers' data.

Remember, the tools and software you choose can be a significant factor in the success of your AI side hustle. Select wisely, and you'll find that these AI assistants can not only save time but also help carve out your path to becoming a passive income millionaire.

Treasure Your Key Takeaways.

As we wrap up this enlightening journey through the world of AI tools and software, let's pause to crystallize the key insights that will anchor your understanding and application of these powerful resources. Embracing AI tools is not just about keeping up with trends; it's about strategically harnessing technology to elevate your side hustle to unprecedented heights.

Adaptability is Key: The landscape of AI tools is ever-changing. Commit to continuous learning and stay flexible to incorporate new and emerging technologies that could benefit your business.

Focus on Strengths: Choose tools that complement and enhance your unique strengths and business model. It's not about having all the tools but having the right ones that align with your vision.

Efficiency Equals Growth: Time is your most valuable asset. AI-driven time and project management tools are not optional luxuries; they are necessities for efficient growth.

Data is Your Compass: Analytics and visualization tools are indispensable for making informed decisions. Let data guide your strategy, but remember to apply human intuition and experience to interpret it.

Personalize Your Customer Experience: Utilize AI in CRM to deliver personalized experiences that build customer loyalty and advocacy, key drivers of sustainable business growth.

Content is Currency: In the realm of online business, high-quality content is currency. AI can help you produce it more efficiently, but the human touch will always be its heart.

Financial Health is Foundational: Whether for budgeting, forecasting, or investing, AI financial tools can provide insights that might otherwise be missed, safeguarding the financial health of your enterprise.

Security is Paramount: As your business grows, so does the need to protect it. Prioritize AI tools that offer robust security features to protect your and your customers' data.

Integration Over Isolation: The most effective AI toolset is one that works in harmony, where each tool seamlessly integrates with others to create a cohesive and streamlined workflow.

Keep these takeaways in your tool belt as you navigate the future of your AI side hustle.

At views AI as not just a lucrative side hustle but a pathway to generational wealth. They are the distilled essence of this chapter—a beacon to guide you as you continue to build, grow, and thrive in the exhilarating world of AI entrepreneurship.41

Chapter 10

The All-Important Low-Cost High-Yield Marketing Strategies

"Artificial intelligence will be part of the home just like electricity." - Jensen Huang, CEO of Nvidia (Interview with VentureBeat, May 10, 2017)

Marketing on a shoestring budget doesn't mean

compromising on impact. In fact, it's an opportunity to

get creative, to truly engage with your audience, and

to find innovative ways to stretch each dollar for

maximum yield.

This chapter is dedicated to showing you the ropes of

cost-effective marketing strategies that pack a punch.

In a digital age dominated by AI, your side hustle

stands to benefit enormously from the clever

application of low-cost, high-yield marketing tactics.

These strategies are not just about saving money;

they're about making every effort count, about

reaching the right people with the right message at

the right time. So buckle up as we embark on a journey to uncover the secrets to marketing your AI side hustle without breaking the bank, yet still managing to score the kind of engagement and loyalty from customers that big-budget campaigns are envious of.

Leveraging Social Media Platforms for Organic Growth

Navigating the bustling world of social media can be daunting, but it's also a goldmine for organic growth. It's where your audience lives, shares, and makes decisions about what they'll support next. This subsection explores how to use social media platforms not just as bulletin boards for your advertisements but as communities to engage with.

We'll discuss strategies for fostering authentic connections, curating content that resonates with your audience, and harnessing the nuanced algorithms of different platforms to amplify your presence without spending a dime on ads.

Content Marketing: Blogs, Videos, and Podcasts

Content marketing is about providing value before you ever ask for anything in return. It's the art of storytelling, educating, and engaging with your audience through various forms of content. In this subchapter, we delve into how to create a content marketing strategy that aligns with your brand and speaks directly to your audience's needs and interests. We'll cover the basics of setting up a blog, creating compelling video content, and launching a podcast—all powerful tools that can establish you as a thought leader and draw customers to your AI hustle.

Email Marketing: Building a List and Engaging Customers

The money is in the list, or so the saying goes. Email marketing remains one of the most direct and personal forms of communication with your customer base. Here, we'll explore the steps to build an email list from scratch, craft newsletters that people actually want to read, and ultimately turn subscribers into loyal customers. We'll also discuss segmentation strategies, automated campaigns, and how to measure the success of your emails.

Community Building and Networking

Behind every successful brand is a community of supporters, advocates, and ambassadors. This subchapter emphasizes the importance of community building and how to foster a sense of belonging among your customers. We'll offer insights into networking both online and offline, creating value-driven community events, and leveraging communities for feedback, support, and viral marketing.

SEO Strategies for Long-Term Traffic

Search Engine Optimization (SEO) is the unsung hero of organic traffic. It's about understanding what your potential customers are searching for and making sure your content is visible when they look. In this section, we'll break down the fundamentals of SEO, from keyword research to on-page optimization and from building backlinks to analyzing your search performance. These strategies are all about playing the long game, investing time upfront for a payoff that keeps on giving.

Partnership and Affiliate Marketing for Broader Reach

Partnership and affiliate marketing can exponentially increase your reach with little to no upfront cost. This subchapter discusses how to find and collaborate with partners and affiliates who share your target audience. We'll look at the benefits of mutual promotion, the ins and outs of setting up an affiliate program, and the power of word-of-mouth that comes from solid partnerships.

Utilizing Free Publicity and Press Releases

Free publicity is like the unicorn of marketing—highly sought after and impactful when captured. We'll reveal how to attract the media's attention with newsworthy stories about your AI side hustle, how to craft a press release that gets picked up, and how to leverage media coverage to enhance credibility and attract new customers.

Cheer Yourself on with Your Key Takeaways Every Day.

Before we close the book on marketing, let's highlight the most potent insights from this chapter. From embracing the dynamics of social media to mastering the subtleties of SEO, we've uncovered the strategies that can take your AI side hustle from the shadows into the spotlight—all without needing a blockbuster budget.

Remember, effective marketing is about being seen and heard in the right places by the right people, and it's entirely possible to achieve this with savvy, targeted efforts that rely more on intellect and creativity than on financial outlay.

Action Items to Nurture an "AI is My Lucrative Side-Hustle Vehicle" Mindset

Cultivating the right mindset is essential as you deploy these low-cost, high-yield marketing strategies. This mindset sees opportunity in every challenge and understands that resourcefulness beats a hefty marketing budget every time. In this final subchapter, we'll give you action items to maintain this mindset, ensuring you stay focused, driven, and ready to adapt to the evolving landscape of AI entrepreneurship. From setting smart goals to reflecting on your progress, these action items are your ongoing commitment to growth, innovation, and the relentless pursuit of success in your AI side hustle.

Chapter 11:

AI-Fueled Profitable Side Hustles & High Paying Jobs

"Just as we teach our children the Aesop's fables, we must educate our AI to understand human ethics and the values of society." - Fei-Fei Li, Co-Director of the Stanford Human-Centered AI Institute (The New York Times, March 7, 2018)

In the labyrinth of entrepreneurship, success stories are like torches; they light the way for others and provide hope that the path ahead is navigable and promising.

This chapter shines a spotlight on individuals whose innovative use of AI in their side hustles has not just yielded success but has set benchmarks for what is achievable. It's a collection of narratives that underscore the transformative power of AI when paired with vision, determination, and savvy execution.

Before we delve into these inspiring journeys, let's address the elephant in the room: the disclaimer. It's crucial to understand that while success stories can be powerful motivators, they are not blueprints for guaranteed results.

Success in business, as in life, is the result of many factors, including hard work, talent, timing, and a smidge of luck. As we explore these tales of triumph, keep in mind that your own journey will be unique, and while there's no formula for assured success, there's infinite value in learning from those who have navigated the course before you.

1. **Two friends used AI and $185 to start a side hustle—they just sold it for $150,000: 'It really does print money'**

Sal Aiello and Monica Powers built their lucrative side hustle in four days — and spent less than $200 to get it off the ground.

At first, they started running their side hustle ideas past ChatGPT, using the generative artificial intelligence chatbot as a starting point for market research. Then, they realized they knew how to ask ChatGPT the exact right questions to get useful answers — and other people probably didn't.

Aiello is a longtime CTO for tech startups, and Powers is a product designer who currently runs a strategic design and branding company called Mascot. In March, they decided to create an AI-powered research tool: Fill out a form about your idea, and the tool would input your answers to ChatGPT in a maximally helpful way.

Reference
https://www.cnbc.com/2023/10/16/how-inexpensive-ai-side-hustle-dimeadozen-sold-for-thousands.html

2. A.I. is making some common side hustles more lucrative—these can pay up to $100 per hour

Nicole Cueto, a New York-based public relations consultant, makes money on the side by helping people plan their vacations — booking flights, making reservations and planning excursions. She also has a profile on travel agent platform Fora, where she earns commissions when clients book hotels and experiences through her recommendations.

In January, when Cueto started her side hustle, she spent five to seven hours planning one day of vacation. Using ChatGPT as a refined, filtered version of Google cuts her "research time in half," she says.

Nicole Cueto uses ChatGPT in her travel advising side hustle. The AI cuts her "research time in half," she says

Reference
https://www.cnbc.com/2023/07/29/how-ai-can-make-common-side-hustles-more-lucrative.html

3. Writing a Best Seller Using AI Tools

Author and blogger, James Clear, uses AI-powered tools like Grammarly and Jasper to help him write and publish blog posts, books, and other content. He has been able to generate a significant amount of income from his work, and he attributes much of his success to his use of AI tools.

James Clear, is the author of Atomic Habits, An Easy & Proven Way to Build Good Habits & Break Bad Ones.

His book is a huge best-seller in Amazon. The book is also the number one New York times best seller. Over one million copies sold.

Reference
https://www.amazon.com/Atomic-Habits-James-Clear-audiobook/dp/B07RFSSYBH/ref=sr_1_1?crid=3MQY20GVR0WEU&keywords=atomic+habits&qid=1699570043&s=books&sprefix=atomic+habits%2Cstripbooks%2C119&sr=1-1

4. AI Content Assistants - The Biggest New Side Hustle

Even as AI may replace human jobs, it can create new ones: Some companies have started hiring part-time content assistants, whose job is to generate blog, newsletter and social media posts using AI-Powered chatbots — and then fact-check the results.

This AI-based gig will be 'the biggest new side hustle,' says expert—and it can pay $100 per hour

Reference
https://www.cnbc.com/2023/06/08/how-to-get-a-side-hustle-as-an-ai-content-assistant-.html

5. AI Prompt Engineer is one job that's currently being tipped to have a bright future is the newly emerging field of prompt engineering.

A prompt engineer is someone who is an expert at getting the new generation of generative AI applications such as ChatGPT or Google Bard to do what they want.

Reference:
https://www.forbes.com/sites/bernardmarr/2023/05/11/the-hot-new-job-that-pays-six-figures-ai-prompt-engineering/?sh=5ed318b77d7f

6. The growing demand for AI data scientists

The most in-demand AI job of 2023 can pay over $200,000 and offers remote opportunities

Data scientists play a critical role in achieving this business goal by collecting, analyzing and interpreting the huge quantities of data from newer AI models to help companies make smart business decisions.

Reference:
https://www.cnbc.com/2023/11/02/the-most-in-demand-ai-job-of-2023-can-pay-over-200000-and-offers-remote-opportunities.html

7. 10 Ai Tool Success Stories (2023)

The demand for AI tools is growing as businesses are looking for ways to automate their processes and improve their customer service.

AI tools can help businesses save time and money by automating tasks that would otherwise be done manually.

Here are 8 real life success stories of starting an AI tool:

Ai Tool Success Stories

1. SkillSoniq ($480K/year)
2. Predis ($12K/year)
4. Enterprise Bot ($1.8M/year)
5. Rytr ($60K/year)
6. Enquire AI ($1.5M/year)
8. Vidon.ai ($72K/year)
9. Live Person ($497M/year)
10. Satalia ($14M/year)

Reference
https://www.starterstory.com/ideas/ai-tool/success-stories

Glossary of Terms

Accountability: The obligation of an individual or organization to account for its activities, accept responsibility for them, and disclose the results in a transparent manner.

Actionable Insights: Valuable information derived from data that can be acted upon to make business decisions.

Affiliate Marketing: An advertising model in which a company pays others (e.g., bloggers) to advertise their products and services and generate sales.

Affiliate Program: A marketing arrangement by which an online retailer pays commission to an external website for traffic or sales generated from its referrals.

AI Assistants: Software or platforms that utilize AI to perform tasks or services for an individual or business.

AI Economy: An ecosystem where AI drives value creation and economic growth, characterized by scalability and reduced marginal costs.

AI Newsletters: Regularly distributed publications that share the latest developments, news, and trends in the field of artificial intelligence.

AI-driven Analytics: Systems that use AI to analyze data and provide insights for decision-making processes.

Algorithmic Bias: Systematic and repeatable errors in a computer system that create unfair outcomes, such as privileging one arbitrary group of users over others.

Algorithmic Processing: The method by which algorithms operate on data to perform complex tasks and analyses.

Algorithms: Sets of rules followed by computers to perform tasks or solve problems, often used in reference to the processes that determine content visibility on social media platforms.

Ambassadors: People who promote or represent a company or brand, typically because they resonate with and want to share the company's message.

Angel Investing: Providing capital for a business start-up, usually in exchange for convertible debt or ownership equity.

Artificial Intelligence (AI): A suite of technologies that enables machines to sense, comprehend, act, and learn, potentially autonomously.

Authentic Connections: Genuine relationships formed between brands and their audiences, typically characterized by mutual trust and engagement.

Automated Campaigns: Marketing campaigns that are set up once and then automatically triggered based on specific criteria or customer behaviors.

Automated Revenue Streams: Income generated through systems and processes that operate without the need for continuous active management.

Automated Trading Strategies: Algorithms or bots used to enter and exit trades according to predefined criteria without manual intervention.

Automation: The use of largely automatic equipment in a system of operation or production.

Automation Tools: Software or platforms that automate various business processes or tasks to increase efficiency and reduce manual effort.

Backlinks: Links from one website to a page on another website, which can significantly affect a site's prominence in search engine results.

Brainstorming: A group creativity technique designed to generate a large number of ideas for the solution to a problem.

Brand Narrative: The story and messaging that encapsulates a brand's values, mission, and purpose.

Branding: The process of creating a unique name, design, and image that identifies and differentiates a product or company.

Bulletin Boards: Online platforms where information can be posted for public view, often used metaphorically for social media sites.

Business Automation: The technology-enabled automation of complex business processes to streamline operations and reduce costs.

Business Model: A plan for the successful operation of a business, identifying revenue sources, customer base, products, and details of financing.

CCPA (California Consumer Privacy Act): A state statute intended to enhance privacy rights and consumer protection for residents of California, USA.

Chatbots: AI-driven programs designed to simulate human conversation, often used for customer service or information acquisition.

Clustering: A machine learning technique that involves grouping sets of similar data points. It's used to find patterns and structures within the data without prior knowledge of the group definitions.

Collaborative Product Offerings: Products or services developed through the cooperation of two or more companies.

Competitive Edge: An advantage that allows a company to outperform its competitors.

Competitive Edge Maintenance: Ongoing efforts to ensure that a business continues to have an advantage over its competitors.

Competitive Positioning: The place a brand occupies in a market or is perceived to occupy in the minds of the target audience.

Compliance: Adhering to laws, regulations, guidelines, and specifications relevant to business processes.

Consistent Content: The creation and distribution of uniform, reliable content that supports a brand's messaging and goals.

Consumer Perception: How customers view and interpret a brand or product based on their impressions and experiences.

Content Curation: The process of gathering information relevant to a particular topic or area of interest to add value.

Content Marketing: A marketing strategy focused on creating and distributing valuable, relevant, and consistent content to attract and retain a clearly defined audience.

Continuous Learning: The ongoing process of acquiring new knowledge or skills through study or experience.

Conversion Optimization: The process of enhancing a website to increase the percentage of visitors who complete a desired action.

Copyright Law: A legal framework that gives the creator of original work exclusive rights to its use and distribution.

Crowdfunding Platforms: Websites where people can raise money for business ventures or projects from a large number of people who each contribute a small amount.

Customer Lifetime Value: A prediction of the net profit attributed to the entire future relationship with a customer.

Customer Loyalty and Advocacy: The outcome of consistently positive emotional experiences, physical attribute-based satisfaction, and perceived value of an experience, which includes products or services.

Customer Service Bots: AI-driven programs that simulate a conversation with human users to provide customer service.

Data Acquisition: The process of collecting data to be used for analysis or to train machine learning models.

Data Analysis: The process of inspecting, cleansing, transforming, and modeling data with the goal of discovering useful information, informing conclusions, and supporting decision-making.

Data Collection: The process of gathering information from various sources to be used for analysis. Methods include surveys, web scraping, sensors, and more.

Data Inputs: Data that is fed into a system for processing.

Data Mining: The practice of examining large databases in order to generate new information or find patterns.

Data-Driven: Making decisions based on data analysis rather than intuition or observation alone.

Deep Learning: A class of machine learning algorithms that use several layers of neural networks to progressively extract higher-level features from raw input.

Delegation: The assignment of responsibility or authority to another person to carry out specific activities.

Democratization of AI: Making AI tools accessible to a broader range of users beyond large tech companies, including small and medium-sized enterprises.

Deployment Environments: The settings and platforms where software applications are released for use and operation.

Design Language: A set of design guidelines that create a cohesive visual brand representation.

Digital Assets: Digital content or online resources owned by an individual or organization, including data, branding, and intellectual property.

Digital Toolkit: A collection of digital tools and software designed to enhance business operations and productivity.

Diversification: The process of a business enlarging or varying its range of products or field of operation to spread risk.

Educating Your Market: Providing valuable information to potential customers to help them understand and appreciate your products or services.

Emotional Anchors: Elements that create an emotional connection between a brand and its customers, leading to loyalty.

Emotional Connection: A bond formed between a brand and its customers based on feelings and emotional responses.

Entrepreneurial Spirit: A mindset that embraces innovation, risk-taking, and the pursuit of new market opportunities for growth.

Estate Management: The process of overseeing the management of one's personal, financial, and legal affairs while alive and posthumously.

Ethical Considerations: Moral principles that influence decision-making and actions within businesses.

Ethical Investing: An investment strategy where the investor's ethical values (e.g., social justice, environmental sustainability) are the primary driving force behind investment decisions.

Ethics in AI: The branch of ethics that examines the moral aspects of AI, including how AI should be used and the impact it has on society.

Feedback: Information about reactions to a product, a person's performance of a task, etc., used as a basis for improvement.

Financial Freedom: Having sufficient personal wealth to live, without having to work actively for basic necessities.

Financial Planning: The process of framing financial policies in relation to procurement, investment, and administration of funds of an enterprise.

Foresight: The ability to predict what will happen or be needed in the future.

Freemium: A business model where basic services are provided free of charge while more advanced features must be paid for.

GDPR (General Data Protection Regulation): A regulation in EU law on data protection and privacy in the European Union and the European Economic Area.

General AI: AI with comprehensive intellectual capabilities that rival human cognition; also known as Strong AI.

Generational Wealth: Assets passed down from one generation to the next.

Google AI Platform: A suite of cloud services provided by Google to build machine learning applications. Known for its user-friendliness and seamless integration with other Google services.

High-Risk Investment: An asset that has the potential for high returns but also a high potential for loss.

IBM Watson: IBM's suite of enterprise-ready AI services, applications, and tools. It is recognized for its powerful natural language processing capabilities.

Ideation: The creative process of generating, developing, and communicating new ideas. It is the initial step in the journey of product or service development.

Inclusivity: The practice or policy of including people who might otherwise be excluded or marginalized.

Industry Events: Gatherings where professionals from a certain sector come together to discuss latest trends, share insights, and network.

Intellect and Creativity: The use of cognitive abilities and imaginative processes to solve problems, generate ideas, or create works with value and significance.

Intellectual Property Rights: Legal protections for creators of original works, including copyrights, patents, trademarks, and trade secrets.

Investment Portfolio: A collection of assets such as stocks, bonds, commodities, currencies, and cash equivalents, as well as their fund counterparts.

Iterative: A process for arriving at a decision or a desired result by repeating rounds of analysis or a cycle of operations.

Keyword Research: The practice of researching common, niche, or trending terms that individuals enter into search engines, used to inform content creation and marketing strategy.

Lead Magnets: An incentive that marketers offer to potential buyers in exchange for their email address or other contact information.

Legacy Building: Establishing assets or creating initiatives that have lasting impact and can be passed down to future generations.

Licensing Proprietary Algorithms: Offering the use of owned unique algorithms to other entities for a fee.

Long-Term Wealth: The accumulation and management of assets over an extended period to achieve financial security and prosperity.

Machine Learning: A subset of AI involving algorithms that improve automatically through experience and by the use of data.

Machine Learning Algorithms: Algorithms that allow computers to learn and make predictions or decisions based on data.

Marginal Costs: The cost of producing one additional unit of a product or service.

Market Demand: The total demand for a product or service in a market at a given price.

Market Trend Analysis: The evaluation of changes and patterns in market behavior over a period of time.

Market Trends: The general direction in which something is developing or changing in a market.

Marketing: The action or business of promoting and selling products or services.

Media Coverage: The dissemination of news and feature articles through the media, which can help increase visibility and credibility for a business.

Microsoft Azure: Microsoft's cloud computing service for building, testing, deploying, and managing applications and services. Offers various AI tools and frameworks.

Mind Mapping: A visual tool that helps structure information, allowing for better analysis, comprehension, synthesis, and generation of new ideas.

Monetization Strategy: A plan for how a business will make money with its products or services.

Mutual Promotion: A collaborative effort between two parties to promote each other's products or services.

MVP (Minimum Viable Product): A product with just enough features to satisfy early customers, and to provide feedback for future product development.

Narrow AI: AI systems designed to handle specific tasks; also known as Weak AI.

Natural Language Processing (NLP): A field of AI that gives machines the ability to read, understand, and derive meaning from human languages.

Neural Networks: Computing systems vaguely inspired by the biological neural networks that constitute animal brains, used for pattern recognition and decision making.

Newsworthy Stories: Information or reports that are considered sufficiently interesting to the general public or a specific audience to warrant press attention or coverage.

On-Page Optimization: The practice of optimizing individual web pages in order to rank higher and earn more relevant traffic in search engines.

Monetizing: The process of converting something into money or earning money from it.

Organic Growth: Growth achieved through a company's existing businesses, as opposed to growth from buying new businesses.

Output Applications: The end-use or function where the processed data or the results of algorithmic processing are utilized.

Passive Income: Earnings derived from a rental property, limited partnership, or other enterprise in which a person is not actively involved.

Perceived Value: The customers' evaluation of the worth of a product or service based on their perception rather than its actual cost.

Personality: The visible aspects of a brand's character that define and differentiate it in the market.

Personalized Communication: Tailoring communication methods and messages to individual preferences and behaviors.

Personas: Fictional characters created to represent the different user types that might use a product, brand, or service in a similar way.

Positioning: The process of establishing a brand or product in the market and in the minds of consumers, relative to competitors.

Predictive Sales Data: Information based on data analysis used to forecast future sales trends and outcomes.

Pricing Strategies: Methods used to set the price of a product or service to maximize profitability.

Privacy: The right of individuals or groups to keep their information confidential and to control, within bounds, what information about them is collected and how.

Profitable Venture: A business endeavor that results in financial gain.

Progress Tracking: Monitoring the advancement of tasks or projects towards completion.

Prototyping: An early sample, model, or release of a product built to test a concept or process.

Real-Time Insights: Immediate, up-to-the-minute information extracted from data to help inform decision-making.

Regression Analysis: A statistical method for modeling the relationship between a dependent variable and one or more independent variables. Used in machine learning for prediction tasks.

Resource Management: The efficient and effective deployment and allocation of resources when and where they are needed.

Resourcefulness: The ability to overcome difficulties or to find solutions to problems by using creative thinking or by making the best use of available resources.

Return on Investment (ROI): A measure used to evaluate the efficiency or profitability of an investment or compare the efficiency of a number of different investments.

Revenue Model: The strategy that a business uses to generate income and profits.

Risk Assessment: The identification and analysis of relevant risks to achieving objectives, followed by the coordination of efforts to monitor, manage, and mitigate those risks.

Sales Funnels: A marketing concept that maps out the journey a customer goes through when making any kind of purchase.

Scalability: The ability of a system to handle a growing amount of work or its potential to be enlarged to accommodate that growth.

Scheduling: The process of arranging, controlling, and optimizing work and workloads in a production process or manufacturing process.

Search Performance: The effectiveness of a website in attracting traffic through organic search results, often assessed using metrics like search rankings, impressions, and click-through rates.

Segmentation Strategies: Techniques used to divide a broad target market into subsets of consumers, businesses, or countries that have, or are perceived to have, common needs, interests, and priorities.

SEO (Search Engine Optimization): The practice of increasing the quantity and quality of traffic to your website through organic search engine results.

Smart Goals: Specific, Measurable, Achievable, Relevant, and Time-bound objectives that guide goal setting and achievement.

Social Impact: The effect of an activity on the social fabric of the community and well-being of individuals and families.

Social Media Campaigns: Targeted marketing efforts to promote content through social media channels.

Social Proof: A psychological phenomenon where people assume the actions of others in an attempt to reflect correct behavior for a given situation.

Stepping Stone: An action or event that helps one to make progress towards a specified goal.

Storytelling: The art of conveying messages or narratives through a coherent sequence of written or spoken words, or through images and sounds.

Strategic Effort: A deliberate and planned set of actions aimed at achieving a specific goal.

Strategic Partnerships: Long-term, mutually beneficial arrangements between two separate companies that have aligned business objectives.

Structured Data: Data that is organized in a defined manner, often in rows and columns, making it easily searchable and understandable by machine learning algorithms.

Subscriber Engagement: The interaction between a sender (usually a business) and the receiver (the subscriber) via email communications.

Subscription-based Models: Pricing models where customers pay a recurring price at regular intervals to access a product or service.

Subscription-based Services: Business model that charges customers a recurring fee at regular intervals for access to a product or service.

Supplemental Income: Additional income that may support one's primary income source, often derived from a side job or business.

SWOT Analysis: A strategic planning technique used to identify Strengths, Weaknesses, Opportunities, and Threats related to project or business ventures.

Task Allocation: The assignment of tasks to appropriate resources or team members.

Testimonials: A formal statement testifying to someone's character and qualifications or to the benefits of a product.

Testing: The process of evaluating a product by learning from the operation or use of the product to see if it meets the requirements.

Thought Leader: An individual or firm recognized as an authority in a specialized field and whose expertise is sought and often rewarded.

Thought Leadership: The position of being recognized as an authority and source of innovation and expertise in a particular field.

Transformative Force: An influence that dramatically alters or reshapes industries or markets.

Transparency: In the context of AI, the openness in communication about how AI algorithms function and make decisions.

Trend Tracking: The practice of monitoring and analyzing changes and advancements in a specific area or field.

Uncertainty: The state of being uncertain; lack of certainty about the future.

Unique Value Proposition (UVP): A clear statement that describes the unique benefits and value of a company's offer, distinguishing it from competitors.

User Experience (UX): The overall experience of a person using a product, particularly in terms of how easy or pleasing it is to use.

User Journeys: The path a user follows across an interface to complete tasks, designed to provide insights into the user experience.

User Research: The process of understanding user behaviors, needs, and motivations through observation techniques, task analysis, and other feedback methodologies.

Value Proposition: An innovation, service, or feature intended to make a company or product attractive to customers.

Value-Driven: Initiatives, activities, or interactions that are centered on delivering genuine value to customers or stakeholders.

Viral Marketing: A method of marketing whereby consumers are encouraged to share information about a company's goods or services via the Internet.

Visual Identity: The visual elements of a brand, such as logos, typography, and colors, that create its overall image.

Workflow Integration: The process of ensuring different software applications work together to automate or streamline business processes.

References

CNBC Article on AI Side Hustle Sale:
Novet, J. (2023, October 16). Two friends used AI and $185 to start a side hustle—they just sold it for $150,000: 'It really does print money'. CNBC. https://www.cnbc.com/2023/10/16/how-inexpensive-ai-side-hustle-dimeadozen-sold-for-thousands.html

CNBC Article on AI and Side Hustles:
Clifford, C. (2023, July 29). A.I. is making some common side hustles more lucrative—these can pay up to $100 per hour. CNBC. https://www.cnbc.com/2023/07/29/how-ai-can-make-common-side-hustles-more-lucrative.html

James Clear's Use of AI Tools:
Clear, J. (n.d.). Atomic Habits: An Easy & Proven Way to Build Good Habits & Break Bad Ones. Retrieved October 23, 2023, from https://www.amazon.com/Atomic-Habits-James-Clear-audiobook/dp/B07RFSSYBH/ref=sr_1_1?crid=3MQY20GVR0WEU&keywords=atomic+habits&qid=1699570043&s=books&sprefix=atomic+habits%2Cstripbooks%2C119&sr=1-1

CNBC Article on AI Content Assistants:
Higgins, T. (2023, June 8). This AI-based gig will be 'the biggest new side hustle,' says expert—and it can pay $100

per hour. CNBC. https://www.cnbc.com/2023/06/08/how-to-get-a-side-hustle-as-an-ai-content-assistant-.html

Forbes Article on AI Prompt Engineering:
Marr, B. (2023, May 11). The hot new job that pays six figures: AI prompt engineering. Forbes. https://www.forbes.com/sites/bernardmarr/2023/05/11/the-hot-new-job-that-pays-six-figures-ai-prompt-engineering/?sh=5ed318b77d7f
CNBC Article on AI Data Scientists:

Browne, R. (2023, November 2). The most in-demand AI job of 2023 can pay over $200,000 and offers remote opportunities. CNBC. https://www.cnbc.com/2023/11/02/the-most-in-demand-ai-job-of-2023-can-pay-over-200000-and-offers-remote-opportunities.html

Starter Story on AI Tool Success:
Starter Story. (2023). 10 AI Tool Success Stories (2023). https://www.starterstory.com/ideas/ai-tool/success-stories

Pexels. (n.d.). New York skyline. Retrieved November 9, 2023, from https://www.pexels.com/search/new%20york%20skyline/

Unsplash. (n.d.). Person sitting at a computer with a lightbulb thought bubble above their head. Retrieved November 9, 2023, from https://unsplash.com/photos/person-holding-pencil-near-laptop-computer-5fNmWej4tAA

Pixabay. (n.d.). Network of interconnected gears and circuits. Retrieved November 9, 2023, from https://pixabay.com/illustrations/network-gears-system-concept-7174083/

Shutterstock. (n.d.). Person sketching out a design on a whiteboard with AI-related symbols and diagrams.

Retrieved November 9, 2023, from
https://www.shutterstock.com/search/artificial-intelligence-
sketch

Freepik. (n.d.). Hand holding a stack of money with a
graph of rising income in the background. Retrieved
November 9, 2023, from https://www.freepik.com/premium-
vector/concept-passive-income-your-path-financial-growth-
human-hand-holding-stacks-coins-money-rain-green-tree-
background-income-growth-concept-flat-vector-
illustration_22959859.htm

Unsplash. (n.d.). Person carefully crafting a logo and
choosing brand colors. Retrieved November 9, 2023, from
https://unsplash.com/s/photos/brand

Pexels. (n.d.). Growing plant. Retrieved November 9,
2023, from
https://www.pexels.com/search/growing%20plant/
iStockphoto. Space rocket launching. Retrieved November
9, 2023, from https://www.istockphoto.com/photos/space-
rocket-launch-photos

Shutterstock. AI-generated art. Retrieved November 9,
2023, from https://gizmodo.com/shutterstock-ai-art-open-
ai-dall-e-1850028869

Unsplash. Marketing campaign. Retrieved November 9,
2023, from https://unsplash.com/s/photos/marketing-
campaign

Getty Images. AI-powered image generator. Retrieved
November 9, 2023, from
https://techcrunch.com/2023/09/25/getty-images-launches-
an-ai-powered-image-generator/

About the Author

Simon Lee is passionate about raising awareness and taking advantage of the once in a lifetime opportunity of the AI Revolution that is upon us.

He is a multi-domain experienced individual with an MBA from a reputable business school and professional qualifications, which include PMP, PMI-PBA, and PMI-ACP certifications from the Project Management Institute. For over 35 years, he navigated the complexities of corporate America, excelling in roles like Senior IT Project Manager, Senior Business Analyst, Senior Researcher, and VP of Finance.

However, beneath his corporate veneer lay a passionate researcher and writer. Even during his corporate tenure, he avidly pursued writing, focusing on genres close to his heart: self-help, health & wellness, the human potential, technology, history, business and politics - and now the AI revolution.

Now semi-retired, Simon (his pen name) has dedicated himself wholly to in-depth research and crafting insightful ebooks and using AI-powered tools to optimize his productivity. A staunch health enthusiast, he's predominantly vegan and engages in daily physical activities, whether it's jogging, working out, or enjoying rides on his electric bike. Weekends sometimes find him at the beach, soaking in the sun alongside his wife.